Flowers of Friendship

When I step into my garden
In the cool of early dawn,
I see a hundred faces
Smiling in the misty morn.

How I love the world at sunrise!
When my flower friends impart
Glistening dew upon their petals,
Friendship's song is in my heart.

Wilfred E. Beaver

Friendship is a fragile thing,
A gossamer web,
A fairy wing,
Yet all the chains contrived by man
Can never bind
As friendship can.

Kathryn Boice

Friendship Garden

Did you treasure as a child
  autographs of cherished friends,
Written in a gilt-edged book,
  names of girlhood schoolmates whom
You remember fondly now
  as you turn each yellowed page?

From my window I can see
  garden flowers now in bloom,
Each plant someone's thoughtful gift:
  lilacs, iris, peonies,
Larkspur, pinks, and columbine.
  Donors' names and flowers blend
When I see them blossoming,
  and I read with tender love
Floral autographs in spring,
  each the name of some dear friend.

Isla Paschal Richardson

*From AGAINST ALL TIME. Copyrighted 1957
and used by permission of Bruce Humphries, Inc.*

Friendship's Perfect Gift

She brought a rose held gently in her hand,
Still fresh and moist with early evening dew . . .
And it was then I came to understand,
To sense her beauty and her charm anew.
Her coming gave fresh hope that stirred my soul,
Assuring me that youth will lead the way;
And through her kindness she has reached a goal
By sharing one rare rose with me today.

I want to keep alive such treasured things:
The little joys like notes from each small bird;
To find that every springtime season brings
The rose, a symbol of love's silent word . . .
Then waiting once again know beauty's art
That comes as quiet April to my heart.

May Smith White

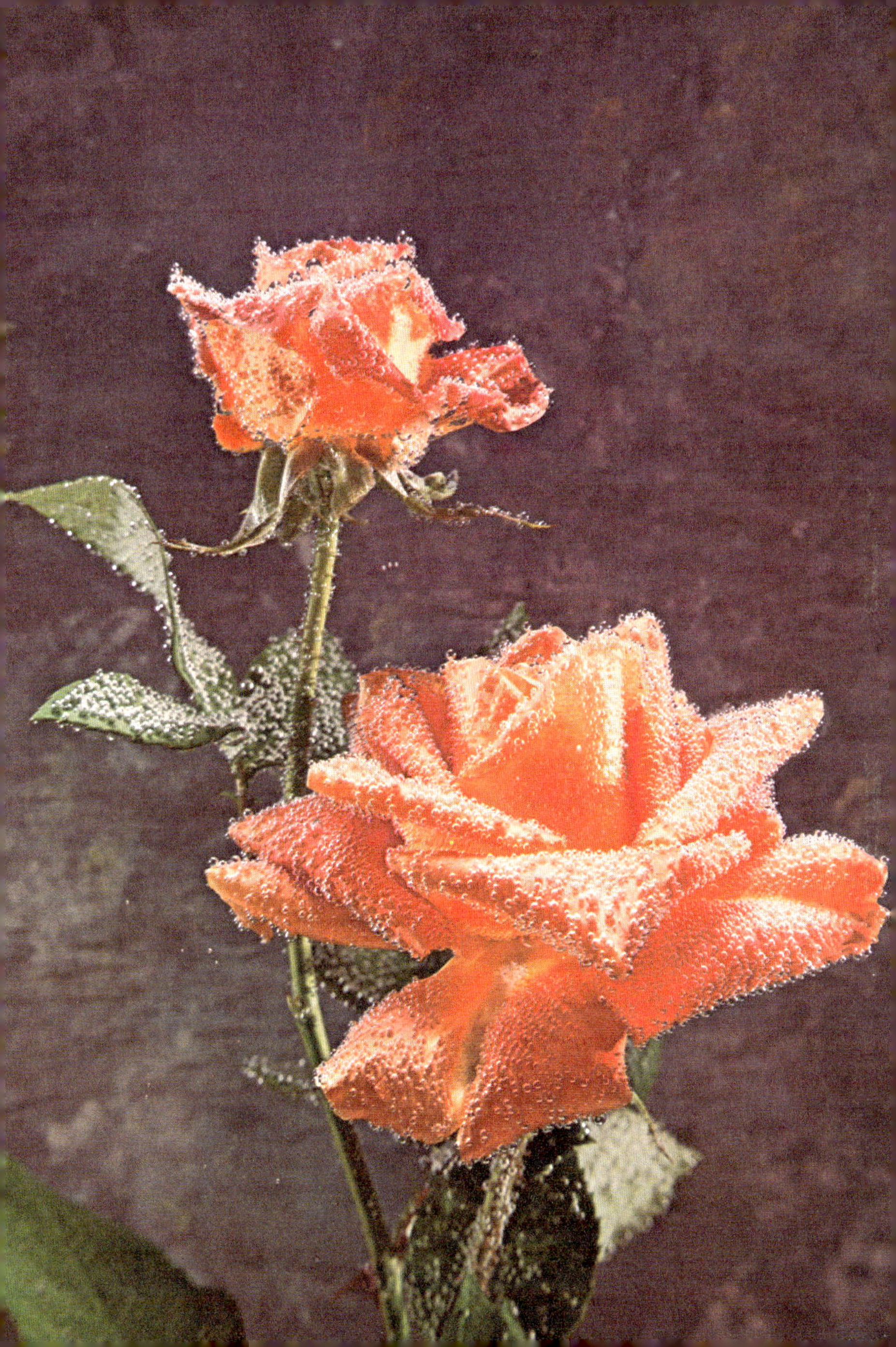

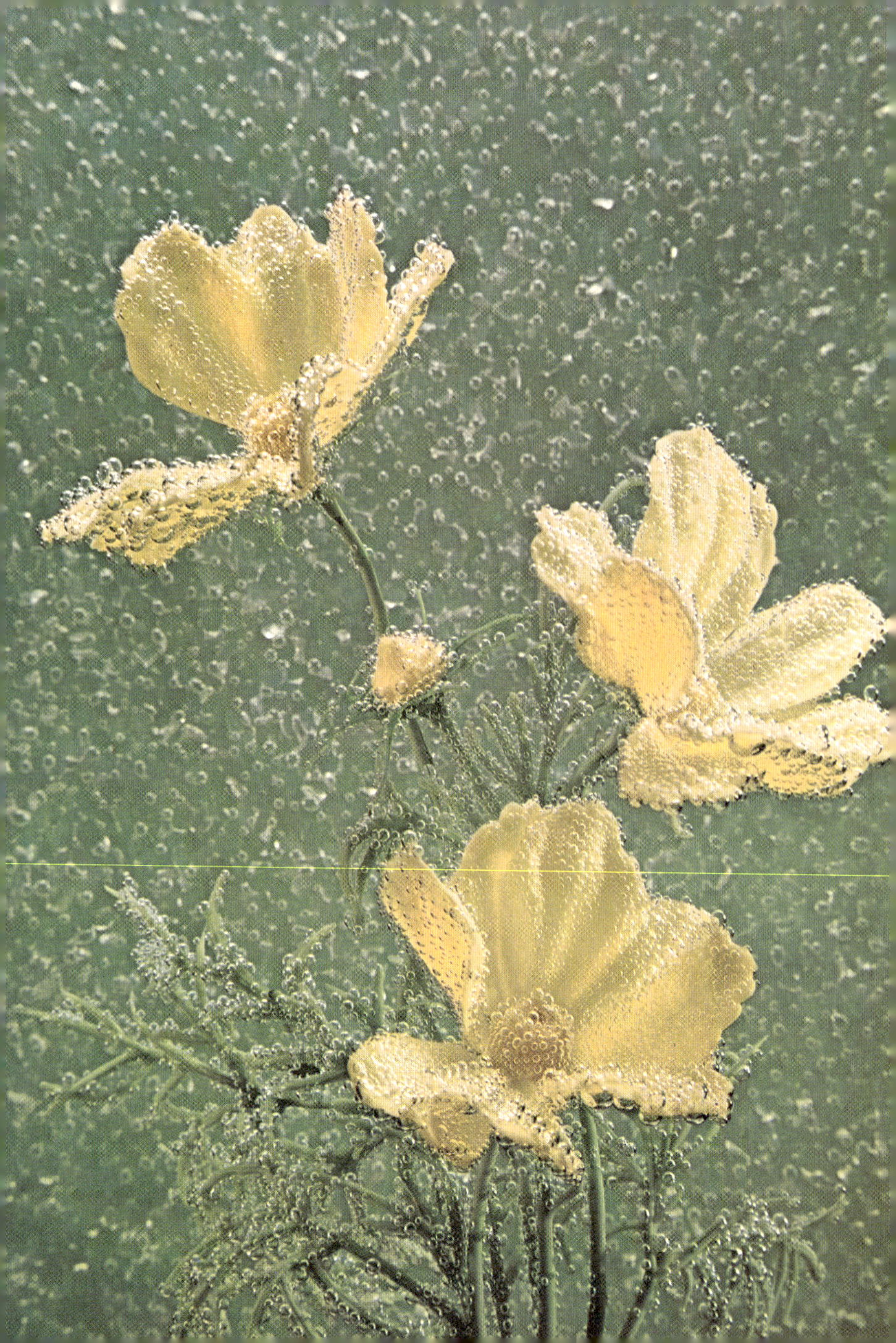

A Precious Seed

So short a while ago I knew you not.
It seemed but yesterday; and then to me
Your voice, your smile, your laughter, came to be
Part of my consciousness and daily thought.
And is it strange that you, with magic fraught
Should merge into my life so suddenly,
Or that, from out of this great mystery,
The bond of friendship should be subtly wrought?

But then it seemed I knew: I cannot say
How came it thus, but yet withal I knew
That you were kindred; and when that first day
We stood among the roses, and there blew
The breath of summer softly on its way,
I found the seed of friendship, and it grew.

Beth St. Clair

Friendship

Friendship is the sun breaking through a cloud . . . It is the fragrance of a flower when a bud bursts into bloom . . . It is the twinkling of myriad stars in the night sky . . . It is the voice of God in the heart!

Author Unknown

Love Gifts

I have a little garden . . .
It's as prized as it can be,
For every seed and bulb and plant
Was a gift of love to me.

Some came when I was ill,
Expressions from a friend.
Oh, the beauty of my garden thrills
And never seems to end.

I even have a plant or two
That are unaccounted for;
Seeds dropped, perhaps, by passing bird
In migration from afar.

Each season has its blossoms,
Each day another bloom,
And though my garden seems so full
I still can find some room
To tuck a plant or two away
That to my garden finds its way.

Helen Corley Cooper

©

Friends Are Like Flowers

   Just as each flower has its own fragrance and its own beauty, so do friends express their own individual beauty. Each one is different and yet, individually, has something to offer along life's journey.

   Each is an expression of the whole, from whom you can learn a part of the completeness of life. Each one is an expression of the unfolding spirit within, enabling you to recognize the oneness with all. From the unification with one another, we are enlightened as to what can be accomplished.

   We learn and benefit from each friend. What we learn from one can be given to another, and what another has learned can be given to us, thus inspiring our progress along the way.

   We become aware that we are individual flowers in the garden of life, and that as such our essence permeates the lives of others. As you behold the perfection and beauty of each flower in an arrangement of roses, lilies or gardenias, so do you see the beauty in each of your friends.

   You derive the full significance of what each has to offer towards your unfoldment, thus helping you to attain complete fulfillment of yourself.

Catherine Plumb

©

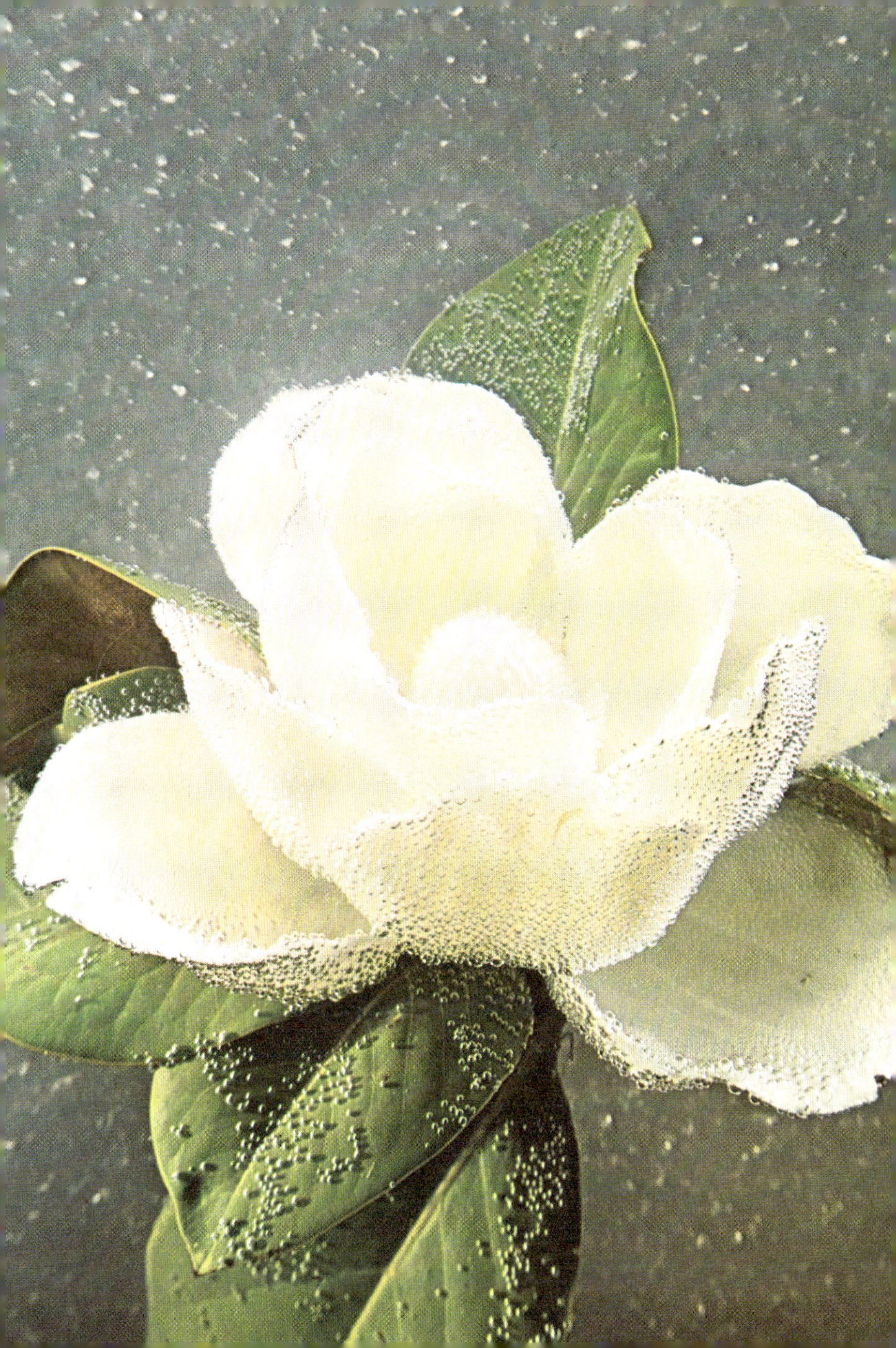

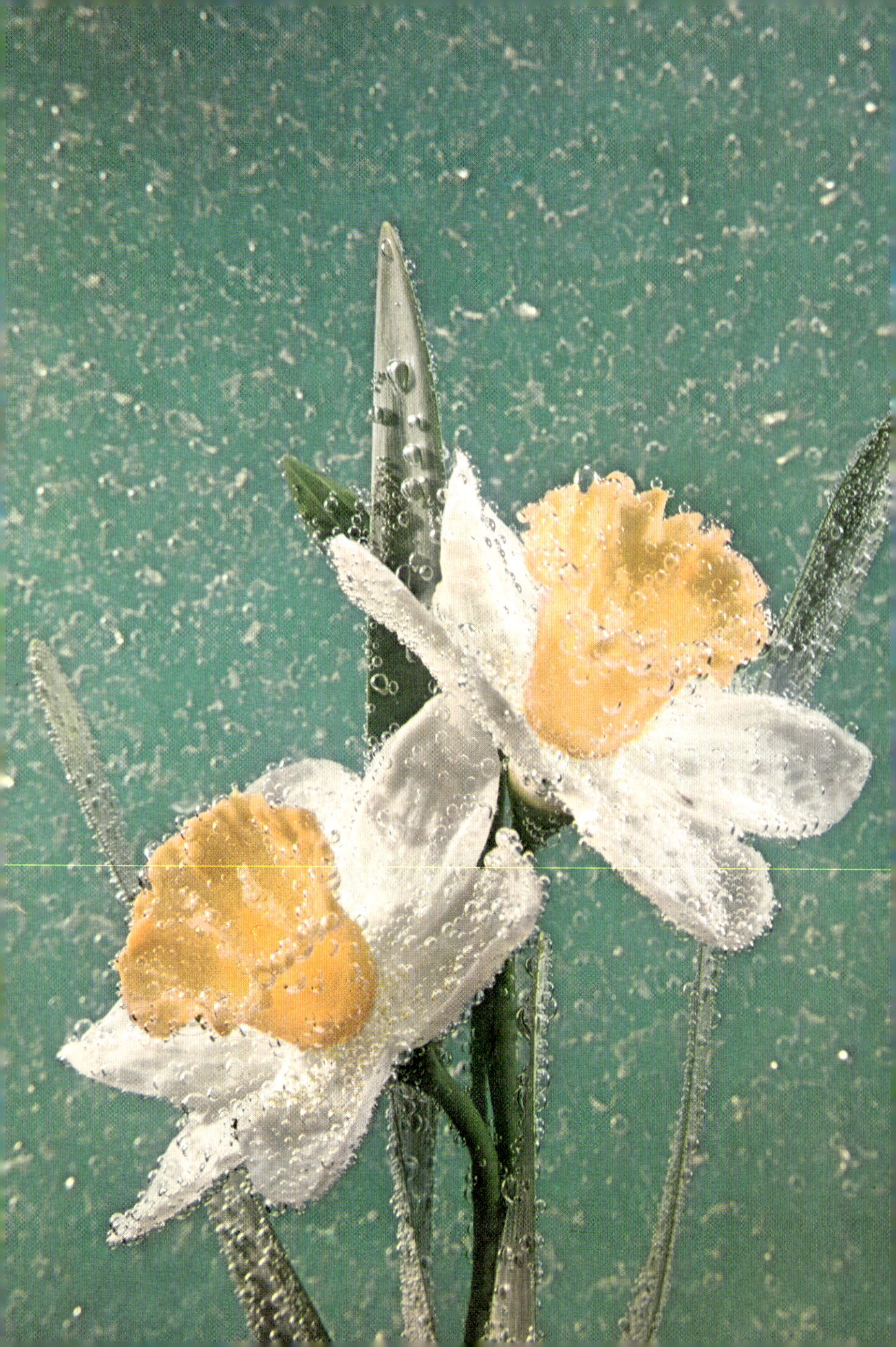

A Singing Bower

My garden thrives in rose and gold;
Its walks are broad and long,
And up and down its wide expanse
Is heard the bright bird song.

But if I had no friend to share
Its beauty and repose,
Its blooms would seem less sweet and gay
For as the blossom grows . . .

So is the heart that sees the joy
Of friendship's bud and flower,
And in the sun of peace and love
Makes days a singing bower.

Maxine McCray Miller

The Love of Friends

Give me the love of friends, and I
Shall not complain of cloudy sky
Or little dreams that fade and die.

Give me the clasp of one firm hand,
The lips that say, "I understand,"
And I shall walk on holy land . . .

For fame and fortune burdens bring
And winter takes the rose of spring
But friendship is a God-like thing.

Vivian Yelser Laramore

*Our sincere thanks to
the author whose address we were
unable to locate.*

Invitation

I'll wax the tables till they gleam
Like newborn hope within a dream;
Will shine the windowpanes and flick
The dust from every mantel brick;
I'll use a fragile china tray
Where violets sprawl in dainty spray.
The room in green as soft as moss,
Reflecting light that falls across
The satin drapes as pale as gold
Will have more charm than it can hold!
I'll serve new bread cut crystal-thin,
And sandwiches most feminine.
Rose fragrance from a single bloom
Will rise like incense in the room,
While thoughts as gay as tropic flowers
Will brighten up the passing hours.
We can be thoughtful, deep, or gay
In all the things we have to say . . .
So visit me at half-past three,
And join me in a cup of tea!

Stella Craft Tremble

©

A Chinese Blessing

I wish you, Friend,
The finest thing
That I can wish for you—
Not health, nor wealth,
Nor luck, but just
A spirit of bamboo.

Bend with the wind
And thus survive,
Though storms may flatten you.
Weep not at fate,
But spring erect
As bamboo thickets do.

Wealth may be lost,
And health may fade,
Yet you'll be wise and true
If you can bend
And you can grow
With a spirit of bamboo!

Helene B. Grouse

©

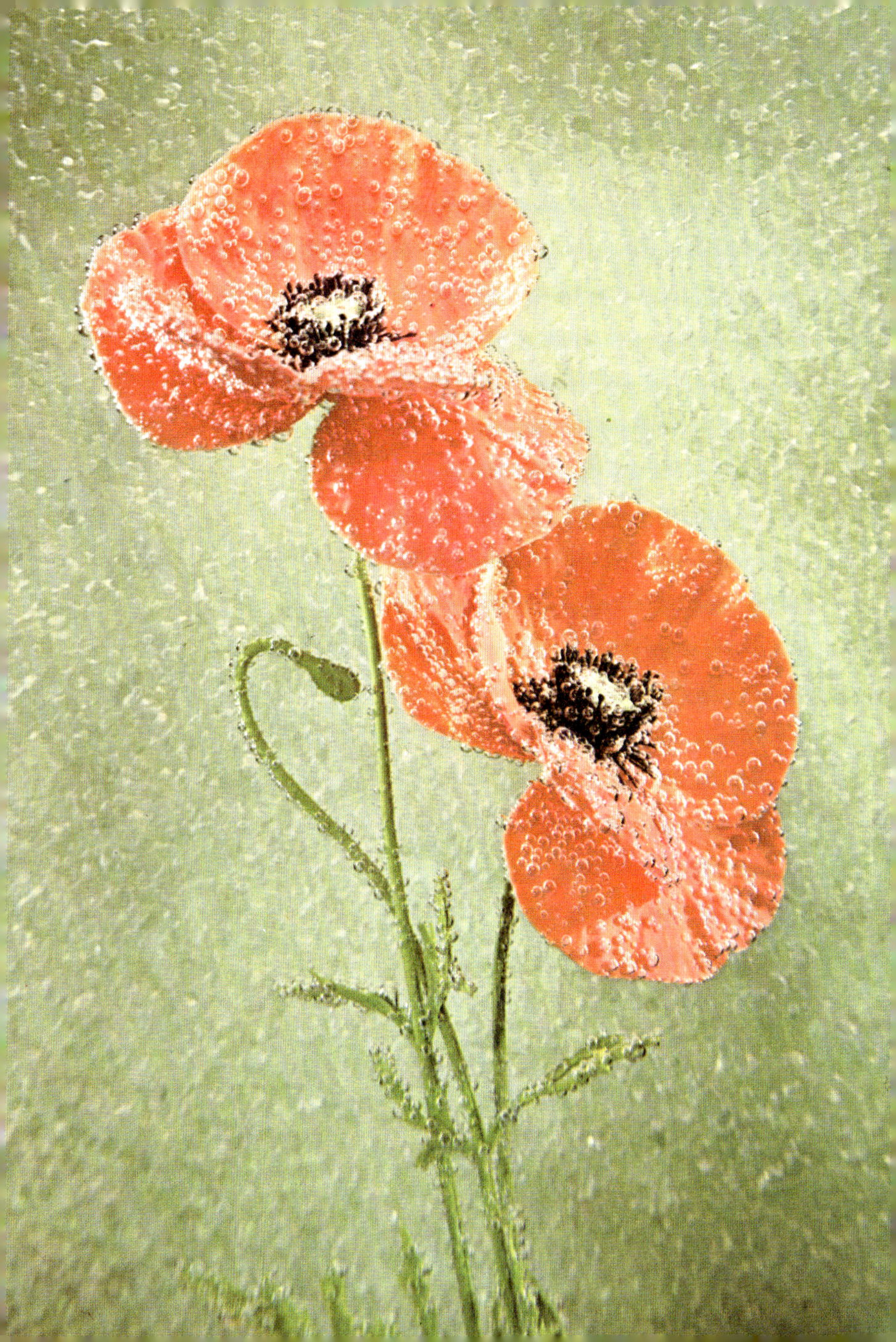

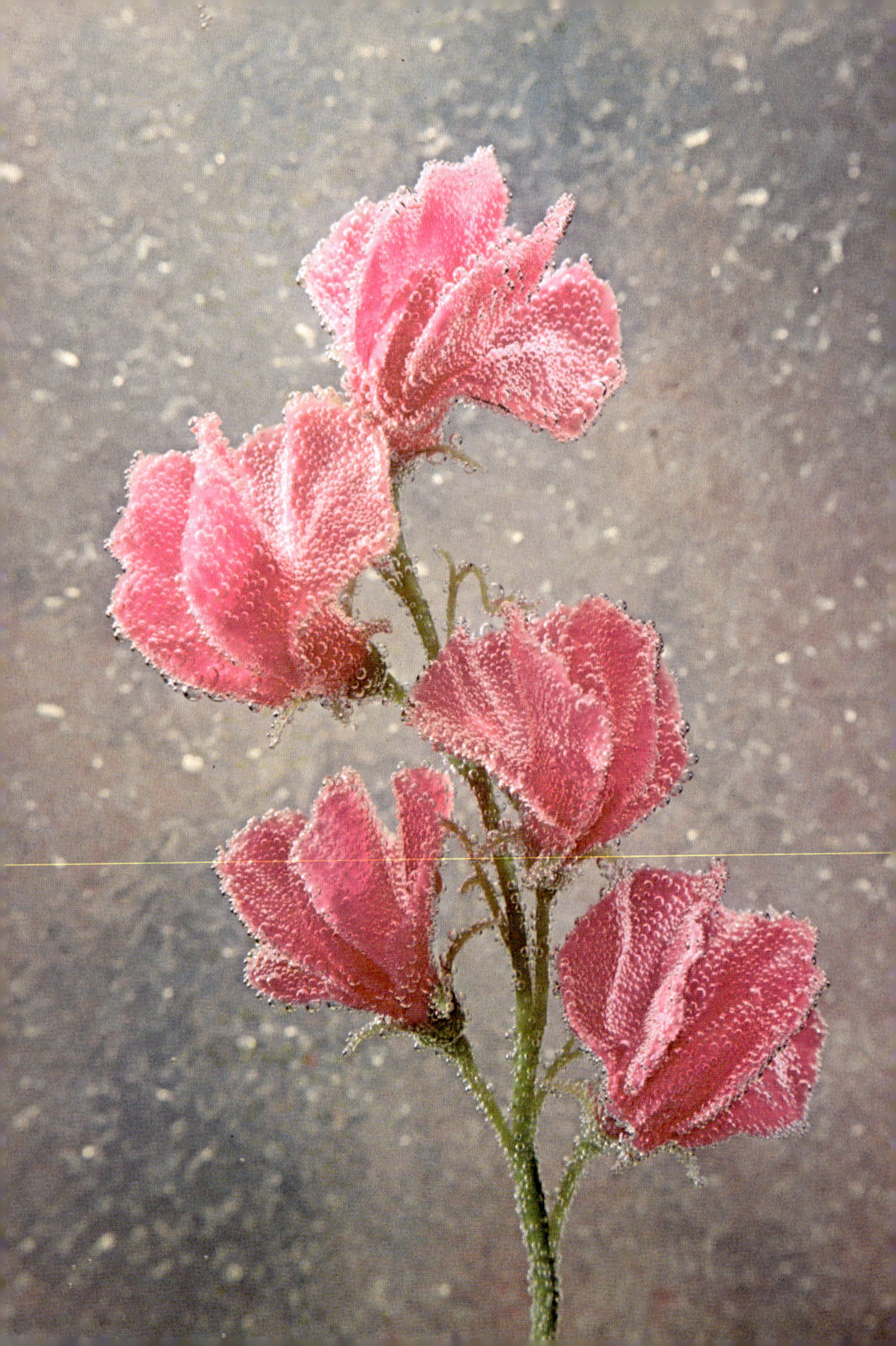

The Whole of Life

Age is a garden of memories,
Flowers we plant on the way,
And the dewdrops we see on the roses
Were tears in some far yesterday.

Age is a tall, slender willow,
Lending its song to the air;
And if one small branch is yellowed,
It dims not the beauty that's there.

Your garden is filled with the flowers
Of all of the kindness you've shown.
Each blossom looks up with the sweetness
Of all of the friends you have known.

The pathway you walk has been gladdened,
The song of the brook is more clear,
The whole of life has been brightened
Because of your presence here.

Pat Whelchel

Around My Door

Around my door that opens wide
Love and friendship twine
And those who step inside will find
A friendly welcome shrine.

Around my hearth where hearts keep warm
Friends gather one by one,
And as the warmth of flames that glow
Love welcomes all who come.

A fresh bouquet of lilacs picked,
Their fragrance to embrace
The many hearts that come to rest,
Or a friend who seeks release.

Around my door which opens wide
Where a garden of flowers abide,
My heart and love are waiting
For loved ones to step inside!

Lydia Dieckmann

Old Friendships

Like well-worn pages in some cherished book,
Old friendships grow more precious with the years;
Like pages long turned yellow with the time,
Old mem'ries are so often stained with tears.

Like winding paths that lead through little dells,
Old friendships are well-worn, but always sweet;
And often thoughts go drifting back once more
To well-known spots where old friends used to meet.

Like flowers pressed in pages of a book,
Old friendships are well-guarded on the way;
Within fond hearts, where nothing can destroy,
Old friendships live forever and a day.

Raymond Orner

Kahlil Gibran speaks...

Your friend is your needs answered.
He is your field which you sow with love and reap with thanksgiving.
And he is your board and your fireside.
For you come to him with your hunger, and you seek him for peace.
When your friends speaks his mind you fear not the "nay" in your own mind, nor do you withhold the "ay."
And when he is silent your heart ceases not to listen to his heart;
For without words, in friendship, all thoughts, all desires, all expectations are born and shared, with joy that is unacclaimed.
When you part from your friend you grieve not;
For that which you love most in him may be clearer in his absence, as the mountain to the climber is clearer from the plain.

On Friendship

And let there be no purpose in friendship save the deepening of the spirit.
For love that seeks aught but the disclosure of its own mystery is not love but a net cast forth: and only the unprofitable is caught.
And let your best be for your friend.
If he must know the ebb of your tide, let him know its flood also.
For what is your friend that you should seek him with hours to kill?
Seek him always with hours to live.
For it is his to fill your need, but not your emptiness.
And in the sweetness of friendship let there be laughter, and sharing of pleasures.
For in the dew of little things the heart finds its morning and is refreshed.

Reprinted from THE PROPHET, by Kahlil Gibran with permission of the publisher, Alfred A. Knopf, Inc. Copyright 1923 by Kahlil Gibran, renewal copyright 1951 by Administrators C. T. A. of Kahlil Gibran Estate, and Mary G. Gibran.

Prayer in a Garden

God make my life a little flower
That giveth joy to all,
Content to bloom in native bower,
Although the place be small.

God make my life a little light,
Within the world to glow . . .
A little flame that burneth bright
Wherever I may go.

God make my life a little song
That comforteth the sad;
That helpeth others to be strong,
And makes the singer glad.

God make my life a little hymn
Of tenderness and praise;
Of faith that never waxeth dim
In all His wondrous ways.

M.B. Betham-Edwards

Blest

I breathe a prayer of gratitude for life,
For all that I have learned and comprehend,
And blest indeed am I if I have earned
The kind regard of an enduring friend.

Harold G. Hopper

©

The Flower of Friendship

Treat a friendship like a flower,
Cultivate it by the hour.
Nourish with kindness, tend with care;
Then when needed, it's always there.
Warmed by smiles, watered with tears,
Friendship will bloom for years and years.

Frank Sherer

©

Give Me a Friend

Give me a friend
  Who'll walk along with me
Through pastures green
  By waters still and deep.
Give me a friend
  Who'll stay the way with me
Though road be long,
  The mountain rough and steep.

Give me a friend
  Who'll share my joys with me,
The perfect summer hours
  When days are sweet and long.
Give me a friend
  To share my ecstasy
When all is bright
  And life is just a song.

Make me a friend
  And I will clasp your hand
And stand by you
  Though everything seem lost.
Make me a friend
  And each mile of the way
I'll love and understand
  And never count the cost.
Make me a friend.

Laura Hope Wood

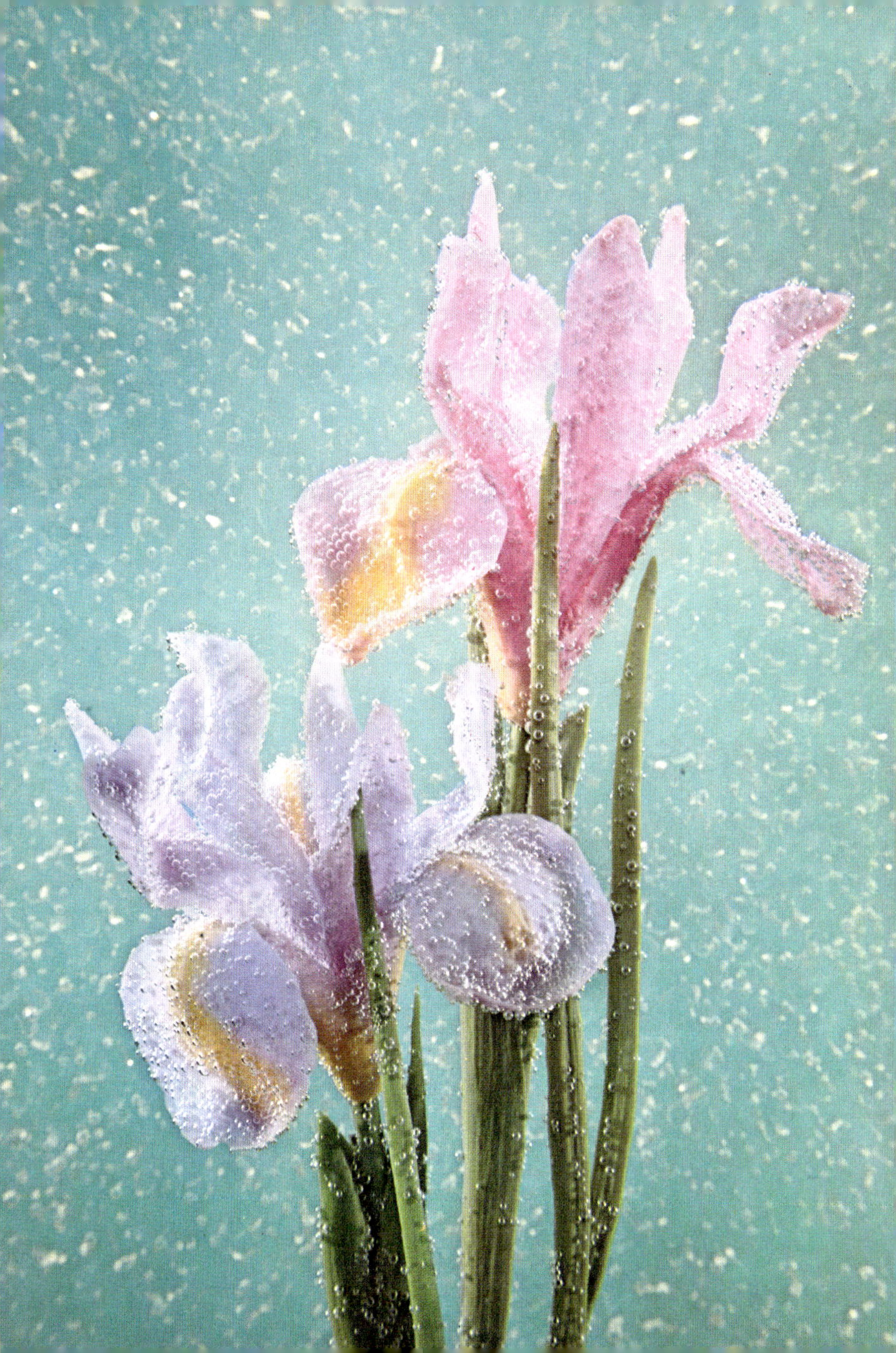

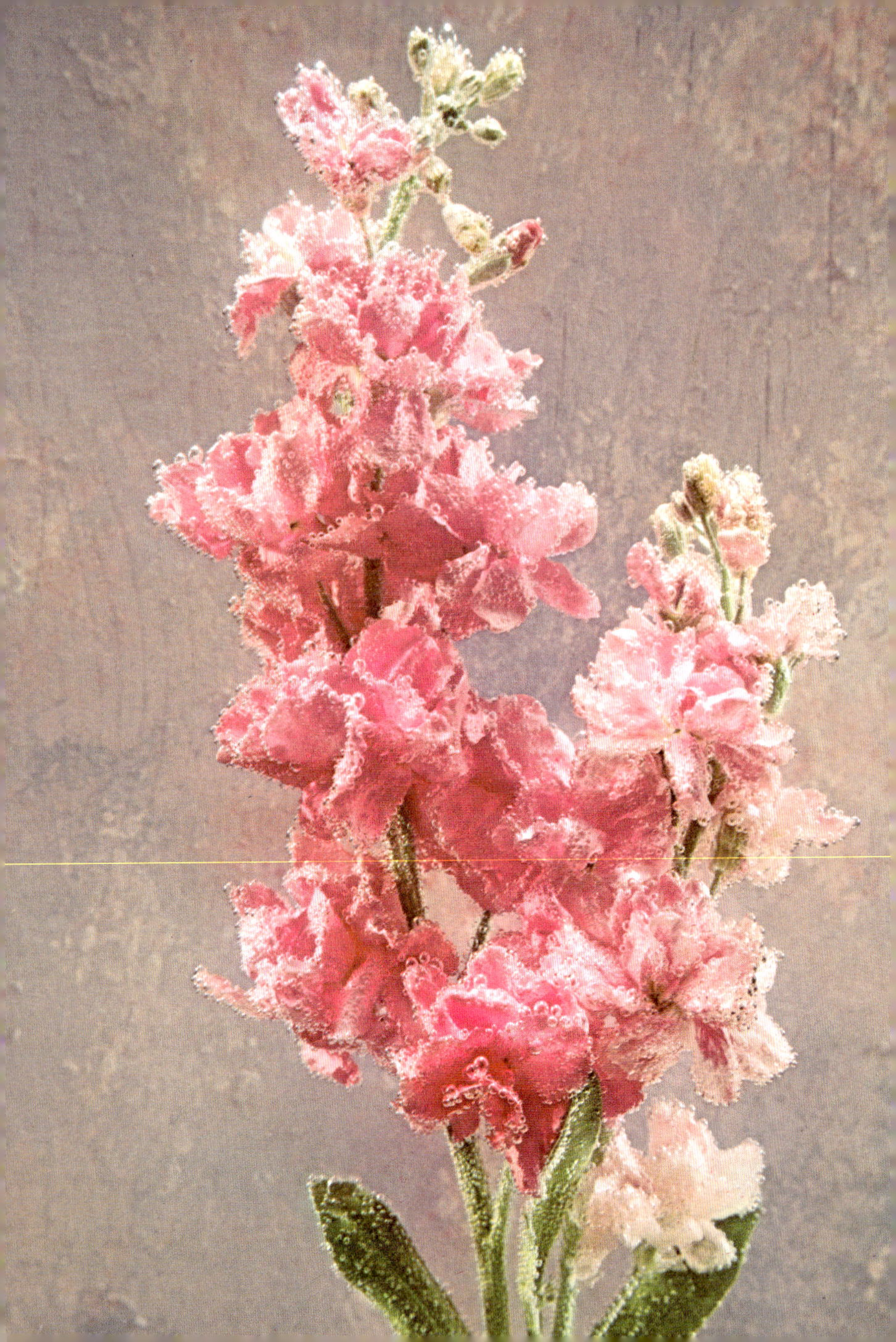

Friends

Friends are like the sturdy oaks that rustle in the breeze when the summer suns are gone . . . Like the boughs of spicy evergreens pressed against our lives to shelter from the wintry blast . . . Friends are like low blooming flowers that break at spring to light our path . . . Like the perfumed roses dropping petals of happiness around our door . . . Friends are like green mosses clinging close to running brooks . . . Like the flowing streams spreading their moisture along the fields and asking no reward or pay . . . Friends are like the shady nooks giving sweet release at evening's hush . . . Like the broad expanse of softest green and copper bronze to delight the eye . . . Friends are like the gentle whisperings of a love divine . . . Forgiving and forgetting without a tinge of blame.

Our sincere thanks to the author whose address we were unable to locate.

Bertha Keiningham

©

My Heart A House Shall Be

My dream has been to build a place to house
The treasures of my journeys, near and far;
A home where many friends may come and browse
In cooling shade, or watch the evening star.
The house shall stand upon a lovely hill
Where pines and oaks a constant vista keep,
And choristers their magic music trill;
A streamlet's murmured song shall lull to sleep.

I bid my friends come now, it's quite complete!
My heart that house shall be, with joys to share;
In garden paths, the blooms waft fragrance sweet,
And memories awaken, fresh and fair
To live forever in this calm retreat;
My thoughts of friends shall all be present there!

Heidi Knecht

©

The Ever-Open Door

What shall I bestow upon a friend? Gay laughter to sustain him when sorrow may bring pain? A bright song of life, belief that winter ends in the glory of spring, a prayer of hope for peace that will ever stay.

What shall I bestow upon a friend? Songs from my heart which I've hidden away? Friendship that flowers, once it enters the heart, spring's eternal loveliness, knowledge that love is a precious thing.

What shall I bestow upon a friend? Fleeting moments of silent blessings? Trust in tomorrow, which is life's hardest task. Faith that each new dawn brings daylight's golden pathways to the ever-open door, belief that God will be with him though all others go their way.

Lea Palmer

Flower-Like Friends

My friends are like a garden, a cultivated garden,
Where many kinds of lovely flowers grow.
They give so much of beauty, such varied kinds of beauty,
Like blossoms, which portray it, row by row.

I have some friends like roses, the perfect long-stemmed roses,
Whose fragrance blesses me when they are near,
While others, sweet like pansies, the deep rich-colored pansies,
Are faithful, velvet-tongued, and very dear.

Some friends, like sturdy asters, the tall and slender asters,
Are strong and firm, but fine and charming, too.
The bridal wreath and lilacs, the white and purple lilacs,
Remind of friends who year to year are true.

Old friends, like gentle iris, the orchid's cousin iris,
Are always there in spring, their love to lend.
But in the small petunia, reblossoming petunia,
I see the constancy of every friend.

Edna Moore Schultz

©

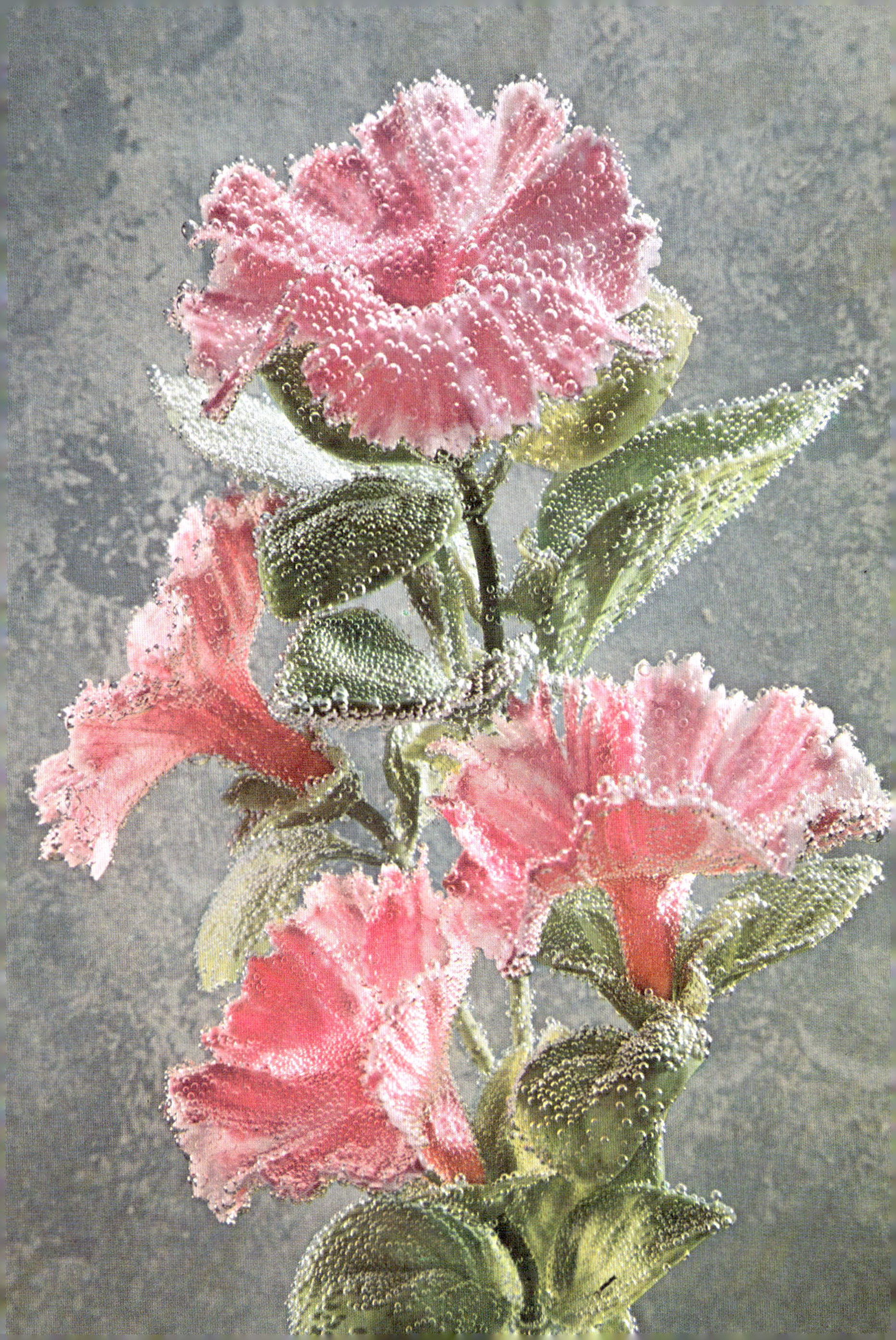

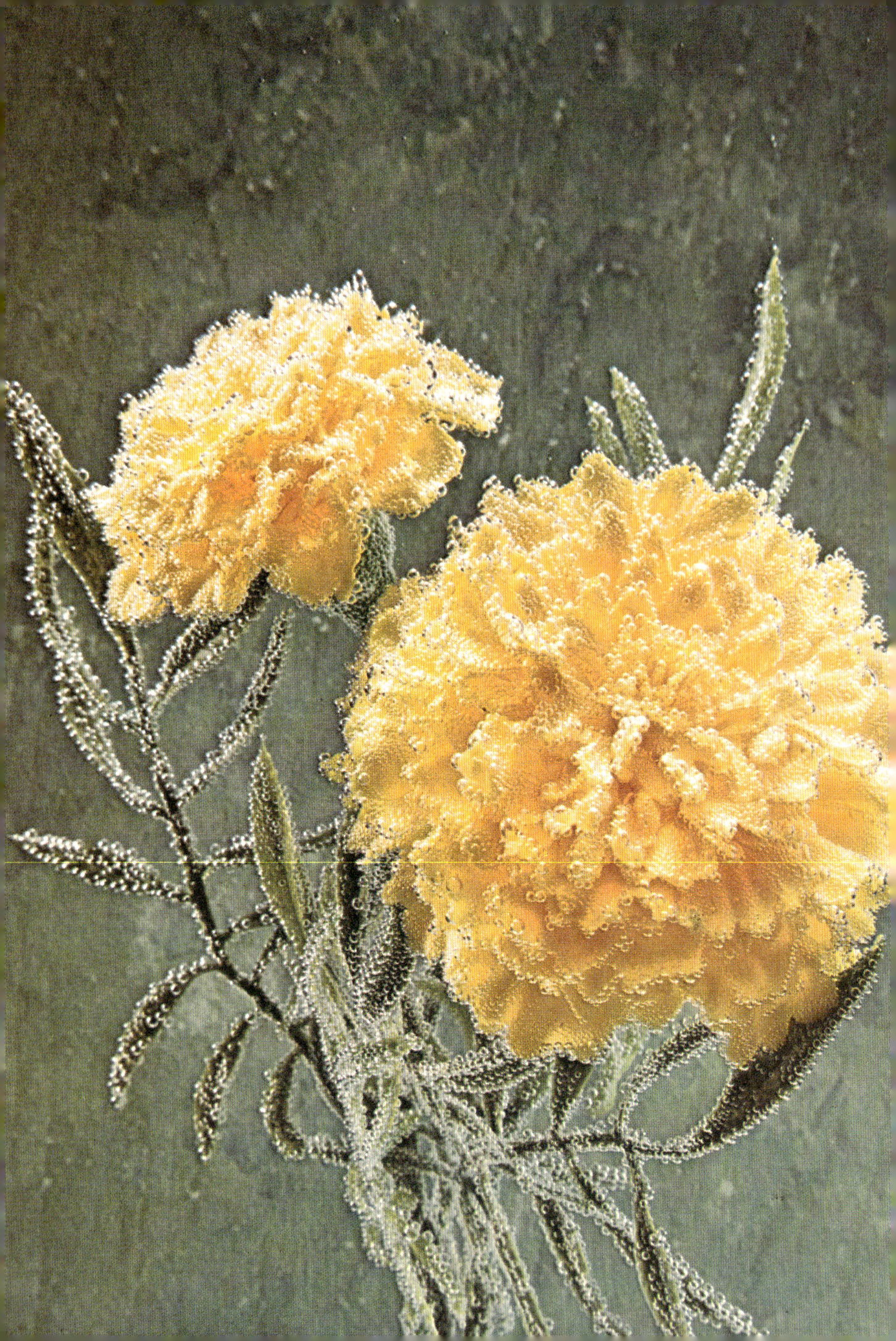

To A Friend

I wish you quiet things—
Sea gulls on upward wings
That seek the sunlit blue;
And silver moonlight through
A wood when night is new.

I wish you joyful things—
Sweet cello murmurings
Of wind on golden hills
And dawn-bright daffodils
And little meadow rills.

I wish you holy things—
A gloried faith that sings,
An eagerness to share,
And every day a fair
Love-lighted time of prayer.

Grace Watkins

Friendly Paths

Before you were my neighbor,
The woodlot was a wall
Of pink and green and silver
With blue sky over all.

But now with you beyond it,
Green arches open wide
Little doors of friendliness
Where well-worn paths divide.

With arms flung wide in welcome,
The quiet pathways smile
In happy, careless fashion
Along each shady aisle.

There is no wall between us,
Since all along the line
Are little doors of friendship
Between your house and mine.

Genieva B. Pawling

©

A Prayer of Friendship

Thank you, God, for friends.
Thank you for the ones who need me,
　giving purpose to my life.
Thank you for those whom I need,
　who teach me gratitude and humility.
Thank you for those who are different,
　that I may learn tolerance and forbearance.
Thank you for the trusting ones, making it
　possible for me to be trustworthy.
And, yes, thank you for those who have
　wronged me . . .
How else am I to know how to forgive?
Thank you for those I love.
They are the true joy in my life.
And, Oh, God, thank you especially for
　each one who loves me,
For while I am loved by someone, there
　is reason for my being.

　　　　　　　　　　　　Doris Locke

Our Friendship

Flowers have filled an aeon of springs,
But they are still as sweet
As the same old song the meadowlark sings
When his conquest is complete.

A beautiful symphony does not grow old
When we have heard it played.
Millions of years the moon's turned gold;
Still its mystery does not fade.

In this same way my friendship with you
Is an ever-growing thing
That will live an eternity through
And still be as fragrant as spring.

Virginia Pritchett

©

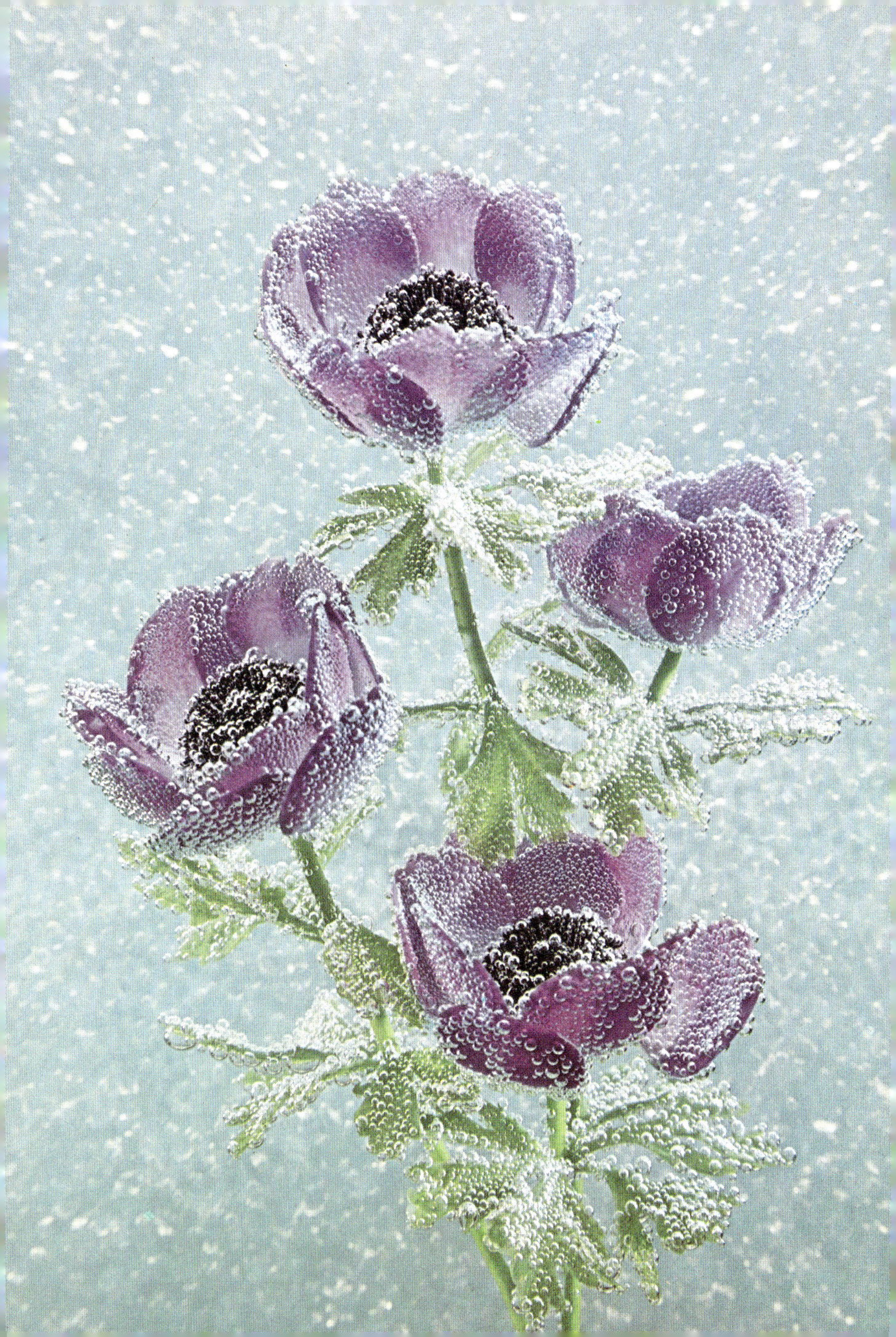

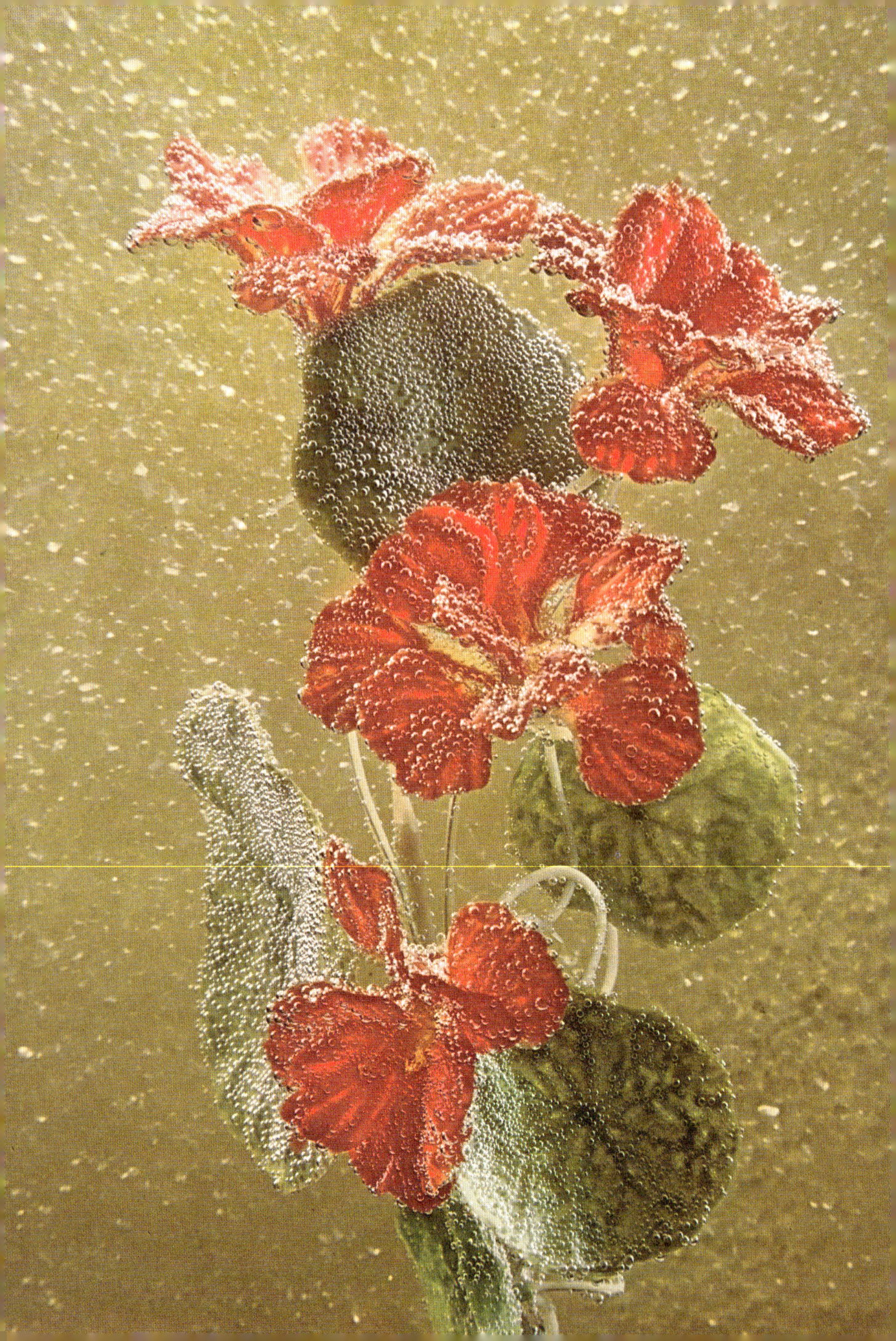

Nasturtiums

Your little gift of flower seeds . . .
I planted in the sod;
I watered them and weeded them,
Then left them up to God.

Today, I'm sending you a gift
To brighten up your hours;
From your little gift of seeds,
Grew all these lovely flowers.

Mary Donato

Wish

Sunlight about you, wherever you are,
And the tree-like peace of the morning star,
Ever within you the song of the thrush—
And sweet rest, friend, when the day sounds hush.

Green roads before you, wherever you walk,
And an old friend near when the heart must talk,
Love's coin be your wealth constantly—
And sunlight about you, wherever you be!

Bert Cooksley

Talisman

Today your friendship is a treasured part
Of all that life may bring through coming years;
And I shall keep it safe within my heart—
A talisman to quiet anxious fears.
And then to live in deeper faith each day
Because you chose to walk the friendship way.

May Smith White

Song For Friendship

I love you, O friend, because you have given
  my heart a new song.
When I was discouraged, a fresh impulse
  to try again;
When doubtful, a new vision of truth and
  victorious faith;
When lonely, you invited guests—the
  great souls,
And made fragrant, immortal friendships.

I love you, O friend, because you have opened
  my eyes to enduring values;
Awakened my giant self—my divine self
  within me;
Because in the garden of my thoughts
You often have uprooted a thistle
And planted in its place a hyacinth.

I love you, O friend, because you have inspired
  in me the flaming, unquenchable desire
To rise and walk out to meet truth and beauty,
  fearless and unencumbered.

Charlotte C. Kinney

©

*Our sincere thanks to the author whose
address we were unable to locate.*

Time goes so fast,
Life asks so much—
No wonder friends
Get out of touch.

But in our hearts,
Deep, true, unseen,
Friendship stays
Forever green.

Mary Darney

©

*Flower photographs by
Louis and Virginia Kay*

Illustrated by Donald Mill